HINDUISM

Hinduism

BY I. G. EDMONDS

Franklin Watts
New York / London / Toronto / 1979
A First Book

Illustrations courtesy of: Vantage Art: p. 3; F.W.I.:
pp. 4, 20; Metropolitan Museum of Art: pp. 9,
10, 27, 28; Sygma: pp. 44, 47; I.G. Edmonds: p.
41; Information Service of India: p. 49.

Library of Congress Cataloging in Publication Data

Edmonds, I   G
Hinduism.

(A First book)
Bibliography: p.
Includes index.
SUMMARY: Covers the history, religion, culture,
and customs of the Hindu people.
1. Hinduism—Juvenile literature. [1. Hinduism]
I. Title.
BL1210.E35   294.5   79–10349
ISBN 0–531–02943–3

CONTENTS

CONTENTS

HINDUISM

THE HINDU PEOPLE

In 1922 workmen digging in a hill called The Mound of the Dead on the Indus River in Pakistan found some burned bricks. Archeologists were stunned.

Ruins made of burned bricks indicated a much more advanced civilization than anyone thought possible in this barren region. Digging deeper, they uncovered the remains of an amazing city that proved to be more than 5,000 years old.

This was not a jumble of mud huts, as might be expected. It was a well-built city, constructed by a highly civilized people—a people unknown to history before this remarkable discovery.

Further digging showed that the people of Mohenjo-Daro (the name of the mound where the city was discovered) had a written language. This was startling in itself. Writing was supposed to have started with the Summerians of Mesopotamia (now Iraq) and the Egyptians along the Nile. Now it seemed that a completely different type of writing developed at the same time as the other two types. Summerian wedge-shaped writing and Egyptian picture writing have been translated. The writing of Mohenjo-Daro is still a mystery.

THE COMING OF THE ARYAS

The findings at Mohenjo-Daro started a search for other "lost" cities along the Indus River. Several were found, including an important one at Harappa in northern Pakistan. These cities were spread out over a thousand miles (1609 km), proving that the empire ruled by these unknown people was a very large one.

Studies of the different levels of the ruins showed that Mohenjo-Daro reached its peak of glory about 2300 B.C. Then it was destroyed by war and fire about 1500 B.C. This destruction came at a time when a mysterious race of people invaded India. Little is known about these invaders except that they came from central Asia, had light skins, and spoke a language known today as Indo-European or Indo-Aryan. This language is the root of the Hindu language of India and also the root of most European languages.

No one knows why these invaders left their central Asian home to spread over Europe. But one branch moved south into Iran and became the ancestors of the Persians. Another branch came through Afghanistan and then into the north of present day Pakistan in 1500 B.C.

These are the invaders historians believe destroyed Mohenjo-Daro. They also believe that the survivors of this great city fled south to become the dark-skinned Dravidian Indians of today.

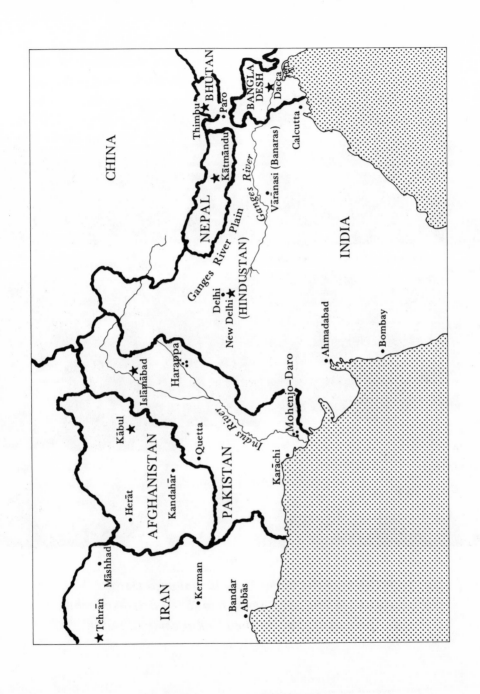

CHINA

BHUTAN
Thimpu ★
Paro •

BANGLA
DESH
Dacca •

NEPAL
Katmandu ★

Ganges River

Varanasi (Banaras) •

Calcutta •

Ganges River Plain

INDIA

Delhi •
New Delhi ★
(HINDUSTAN)

Harappa •

Ahmadabad •

Bombay •

Islamabad ★

Kabul ★

AFGHANISTAN

Quetta •

PAKISTAN

Mohenjo-Daro •

Indus River

Herat •

Kandahar •

Karachi •

IRAN

Kerman •

Bandar
Abbas •

Tehran ★   Mashhad •

Ruins of the Great Bath at Mohenjo-Daro.
The city of Mohenjo-Daro may have been destroyed when
the Aryan ancestors of the Hindus came to India.

The newcomers called themselves *Aryas,* which means nobles. They settled along the Indus River. The nearby Persians called them *Hindhus* (people of the Indus). Later the Greeks, who invaded this land under Alexander the Great, dropped the hard "h" sound from this word. In their tongue it became *"Indic,"* from which we get our word "India."

In time the Aryas moved into northern India, settling twelve small kingdoms along the Ganges River plain. The Persians called this region Hindustan, or "Home of the Hindus." These people were the ancestors of the present day Hindus.

RELIGION OF THE HINDUS

When the Aryas came to India they brought the seeds of the religion that became Hinduism. History calls this the Vedic period because what we know of it comes from the *Vedas.* The Vedas are religious books of knowledge, the oldest of which is the *Rig-Veda.* It was written down in 1000 B.C., but existed in oral form before this.

The Vedic Hindus worshipped gods of nature who represented the sun, moon, fire, and water. This early religion slowly changed as elements of the native (Mohenjo-Daran) religion seeped into the Aryan beliefs. In addition, the growth of philosophy made other changes that eventually brought about modern Hinduism.

Today, Hinduism is the world's third largest religion—after Christianity and Islam. Estimates claim that Hinduism has over 524 million followers.

Of this number, 522 million live in Asia. There are 533,000 in South America, 640,000 in Oceania (islands of the Pacific), about 350,000 in Europe, and 75,000 in the United States.

Hinduism is the only one of the great religions that does not have an historic founder. Moses founded Judaism. Christ is the father of Christianity. Mohammed gave Islam to the world. Hinduism, however, originated in the Vedas (books of knowledge) handed down from a supreme spirit to early priests.

Many changes have come into Hinduism since its Vedic days, and many different sects and beliefs have evolved. However, there are certain things that are common to all the different Hindu sects. It is this basic thread of beliefs that makes all of these different sects a part of Hinduism, even though many of their practices differ.

THE CREATOR SPIRIT

Hinduism teaches that each living body is built around an eternal soul. These souls were originally thrown off like sparks from Brahma, the creator spirit of the universe.

Each soul then, is really a part of the creator, and it is the duty and the desire of each soul to someday return to its creator. But this is not possible because these souls have become soiled by the sins, desires, and impurities of the world. They must cleanse themselves before they can return to Brahma, for the creator spirit is absolutely pure.

This is so difficult that no one can expect to purify his or her soul in one lifetime. Each soul is forced to be reborn again and again until it can gradually purify itself enough to return to its creator.

Hindus compare this cycle of rebirths to a wheel that goes around and around. They call it *samsara,* The Wheel of Life. It is called *moksha* when the cleansed spirit finally gains release from this cycle of rebirths. It then re-enters Brahma for an eternity of happiness and bliss.

BRAHMAN

Brahman is the supreme spirit of all creation. It is perfect and unchanging, and is neither male nor female. Brahman is accepted without question. It cannot be described in earthly terms because the earth is impure. To describe Brahman in earthly words would imply that the supreme spirit is impure itself.

Brahman created the Hindus gods. There are hundreds of these—but three stand above all the others, forming what is commonly known as the Hindu Triad. They are Brahma the Creator of Life, Vishnu the Preserver of Life, and Siva the Destroyer of Life.

BRAHMA THE CREATOR

Brahma—one of the gods that Brahman created out of itself—is the creator of the world. As such, Brahma's work is done. He has nothing to do with the world anymore, and is a misty figure to the average Hindu today. In their daily lives, Hindus turn most often to Vishnu and Siva.

Hindu literature has a number of stories about how the world was created. The oldest is in the *Rig-Veda.* Monier Monier-Williams, a noted Indian Scholar, translates it in this manner:

In the beginning there was neither naught nor aught,
Then there was neither sky nor atmosphere above. . . .
Then there was neither death nor immortality.
Then there was neither day, nor night, nor light, nor
   darkness.
Only the Existent One (Brahma) breathed calmly. . . .
Next all was water, all a chaos indiscrete.
Then turning inward, he (Brahma) by self-development
   grew.
First in his mind was formed Desire, the primal germ
Productive, which the wise, profoundly searching, say
Is the first subtle bond, connecting Entity with Nullity.

In calling Brahma "he," the translator is in error. Brahma
is neither male nor female. We may compare this hymn with
Genesis in the King James version of the Holy Bible:

In the beginning God created the heaven and the earth.
And the earth was without form, and void; and darkness
was upon the face of the deep. And the Spirit of God moved
upon the . . . face of the waters. . . .

VISHNU THE PRESERVER

Vishnu is the second of the three gods of the Hindu Triad. He
is the most loving, forgiving, and ever watchful for the welfare
of his worshippers. He has four arms and is black. His worship-

A bronze statue of a
fish avatar of Vishnu.

pers are called Vaishnavas. Vishnu is said to have a thousand names. These come from his many *avatars*. An avatar is an earthly form used by a god to help mankind find salvation. In worshipping Vishnu, the Hindu may choose any of these many avatars or Vishnu himself. Vishnu's two most popular avatars are Rama, hero of the epic poem *The Ramayana,* and Krishna, whose ideals are told in the *Bhagavad-Gita.*

SIVA THE DESTROYER

Siva is a very popular god. Although he is called the Destroyer, his followers—called Shaivas—believe Siva destroys only to rebuild again. This makes him also a Giver of Life as well as a Destroyer. In paintings Siva appears as a beautiful man, but in the temples he is represented by a stone image called a *lingam.* This image is in the form of the male sexual organ. It symbolizes Siva's role as a Giver of Life.

Shaivas are divided into many different sects. Some Shaivas are ascetics (people who torture their bodies to gain religious merit).

FOLLOWERS OF MANY BELIEFS

There is no unifying creed in Hinduism. Followers may select any one of the many gods as their personal god, or they may worship several. They may even worship in other religions without

A bronze statue of Siva
made in the late 10th century.

ceasing to be Hindus. However, to be a Hindu there are certain things that one must believe in and live by. These are:

1. A belief in *karma,* the result of one's good and bad deeds in life.
2. A belief in *dharma,* the traditions of Hinduism.
3. A belief in Brahma, Vishnu, and Siva.
4. A belief that the soul is reborn after death.
5. Reverence for the sacred Vedas.
6. A belief that the soul can, through a religious life, liberate itself from the Wheel of Life.
7. Reverence for an ascetic religious life.

It is important to remember that although Hindus may worship many gods, they are really monotheistic in that they believe in a single god. This is because all the Hindu gods, like everything else in creation, comes from Brahman. So, regardless of the god to whom the worship is directed, the worship is really toward Brahman.

Brahman, as the supreme spirit of creation, does not punish wickedness nor does it reward goodness. Each living thing creates its own rewards and punishments through karma.

HINDU WAYS TO SALVATION

The Hindu soul must be cleansed of earthly sins before it can return to Brahma. This is extremely difficult at best, but is made even harder because the soul may add new sins in each new life. A person can in fact go backward instead of forward in the search for salvation. This is due to *karma* which rules what each person will be in his or her next life.

KARMA AND REBIRTH

A person's karma is formed by his or her good and bad deeds and by the religious merits gained in each life. A person's merits and demerits are averaged for a lifetime. If the merits outweigh the demerits, then a person has a good karma. If the bad deeds or demerits are greater than the good, then a person can have a bad karma.

Karma is formed as the cause and effect of all that happens in one's life. This karma controls what a person will be in his or her next life. A king with a very bad karma may be reborn a slave in his next incarnation. In the same way, a beggar may be reborn a king. It all depends upon one's karma. The sorry state a person with a bad karma has in the next life is not a punishment. Neither is a good rebirth a reward. Both are simply the result of karma formed by one's own actions.

Rebirth has many names. It has been called reincarnation, metempsychosis, and transmigration of souls. In the Hindu belief, the human soul does not necessarily have to be reborn in a human body. A person with a very bad karma may be reborn as an animal, or even as an insect.

THE DEVOUT FLY

There is a Hindu story of a fly that lived in a temple of Siva in Banaras, the sacred city of India. This fly bothered no one, and often buzzed about the more than one hundred stone symbols of Siva in the temple. This devotion to the god built such good karma for the devout fly that it was reborn as the sage Pulsha, a famous teacher of his time.

Another story tells of a weaver who offended Siva. This weaver spun cloth of great beauty and was richly rewarded for his work. Yet he refused to give money to repair the god's temple.

Siva was angry. He decreed that the weaver should never again profit from his skill. And so it happened. Each time the weaver was paid for his work thieves stole the money. This happened no matter how cleverly the weaver hid his gold.

The weaver prayed to Vishnu for help. The kindly god replied that one god could not undo the curse of another god. The weaver was advised to give up his work and become a beggar. Then he would have nothing anyone could steal.

The weaver hated the thought of this. He loved his work. However, he disliked the fact that his work was making thieves rich. So the next time he was paid, he rushed out into the street and gave the gold to the first person who came by. It happened to be a starving old woman.

The weaver was startled by the look of gratitude she gave him. As time went by, he continued to give his payments to the poor. At first this was done solely to cheat the robbers, but he gradually came to take pleasure in the gratitude of those he helped, and became content just to help others. This impressed Siva, who finally lifted the curse. Even so, the weaver continued to give most of his gold to the poor. This built him such good karma that he was reborn a king with a treasury filled with gold.

HINDU HEAVENS
AND HELLS

There were no heavens or hells in ancient Hinduism. There were only the good and bad lives directed by karma. In today's popular Hinduism, however, there are heavens and hells. A dead person's soul is examined by Yama, judge of the dead. He may send a soul to heaven or hell for a temporary time.

Even so, a person is still a prisoner of his or her karma. The soul must be reborn, for the Wheel of Life must keep turning until the soul is pure enough to return to the spirit of creation.

SALVATION THROUGH YOGA

Good deeds alone are not enough to purify the soul. Certain religious duties and rituals may also help. One action that aids in developing good karma is *yoga*. Yoga means "union." In this case, it means union of the human mind with Brahman.

Yoga is a form of deep meditation that is aided by certain positions and controls of the body, as well as control of the mind. The purpose of yoga is to turn the mind inward and permit the mind to discover itself. Ramakrishna, a great teacher, used a story to illustrate this.

A man awoke at midnight and craved a smoke. But he had no fire to light the tobacco. So he took a candle, which he had left burning beside his bed, and went to a friend's house. He woke his friend and asked for a light. The angry man replied, "Why ask me for a light when you hold fire in your hand?"

It is the same with those who seek salvation, the teacher said. The things one needs for salvation are within one's own self. These each person must seek and find.

THE SEEKER AFTER TRUTH

The *Bhagavad-Gita,* one of the most beloved Hindu scriptures, describes the perfect disciple of yoga. The god referred to here is Krishna, an avatar of Vishnu who returned to earth to help mankind.

> The man who aims at that supreme condition
> Of perfect yoking with God
> Must first of all be moderate in all things,
> In food, in sleep, in vigilance, in action,

In exercise and recreation. Then
Let him, in seeking God by deep meditation,
Abandon his possessions and his hopes,
Betake himself to some secluded spot
And fix his heart and thoughts on God alone . . .
. . . And then let him sit
Firm and erect, his body, head and back
Straight and immovable, his eyes directed
Toward a single spot, not looking around,
Devoid of passion, free from anxious thought,
His heart restrained, deep in meditation . . .
He whose senses are well controlled
Attains to sacred knowledge . . .
Quietness in mind is the state of the Supreme.
He who, intent on meditation,
Joins his soul with the Supreme, is like a flame
That flickers not when sheltered from the wind.

THE HINDU CASTE SYSTEM

Hindu society has always been strictly segregated. The different levels of society—called castes—do not mix. This rigid separation of people is the result of dharma and karma.

Dharma is one of the basic beliefs of Hinduism. There is no equivalent word in English. Charles Francis Potter in his book, *The Faiths Men Live By,* explained dharma in this way: "When a Westerner says a certain thing 'just isn't done,' a Hindu would say that to do such things 'would break dharma.' "

Dharma, then, is sometimes likened to tradition. One dictionary defines it as duty. Another calls it custom. Yet a Hindu, while admitting that dharma is something *like* these things, would add that none of them explains exactly what dharma really is. It is spiritually more than tradition, duty and custom. Only a Hindu can fully understand the subtle difference.

Dharma teaches that if something has always been a certain way, it should continue to be that way. And, since each person's position in life is due to his or her own actions in a previous life, karma teaches that we should accept this.

So if one is born into a certain station in life, he or she should stay there. This is decreed by both dharma and karma. Therefore, it is a sin to try to move out of one's place—or caste—in life.

THE CASTES

There are four castes or levels of society, plus two groups outside the castes. The highest caste is the Brahmin. Brahmin means Brahman. It is spelled differently to avoid confusion with Brahman, the Supreme Spirit. All castes come from Brahma the Creator, but from different portions of his body. The Brahmin comes from Brahma's head. Therefore, Brahmins are held to be the voice of the Supreme Spirit and are considered the priestly class. They are also teachers and keepers of the sacred wisdom. Today, while many are still priests and teachers, economics has forced many Brahmins to go into business and government.

The second caste is the warrior class. In times past, it furnished the kings and soldiers. Merchants, artisans and farmers make up the third caste. Manual workers form the fourth and lowest caste. Each caste forms a separate division of society. People from different castes may not mix, for a person of higher caste is considered to be polluted by associating with a person of lower caste.

Finally, there are the two groups outside the caste system. One is for foreigners of all kinds. They receive special treatment. The other "outcaste" group is called the "Untouchables." People in this lowest caste are not considered human, and are denied any part in Hindu rites. They must do the work no one else wants to do, and are always kept separate from people of higher castes.

MAHATMA GANDHI AND THE UNTOUCHABLES

Untouchability was outlawed in the Indian Constitution of 1947. This was largely a result of the work of Mahatma Gandhi (1869–1948), the Indian leader who led the movement for Indian independence from Britain.

Gandhi was both a political and spiritual leader for Indian people. However, his spiritual leadership was based on the example of his own humble life. Except for trying to stamp out Untouchability, he did not try to change Hinduism. In fact, we can see Gandhi's deep reverence for Hinduism through his struggle to free India from Great Britain. Instead of fighting, Gandhi sought his goal through peace and self-denial.

In his book, *Young India* (1931), Gandhi wrote, "Having flung aside the sword, there is nothing except the cup of love which I can offer to those who oppose me. It is by offering that cup that I expect to draw them close to me."

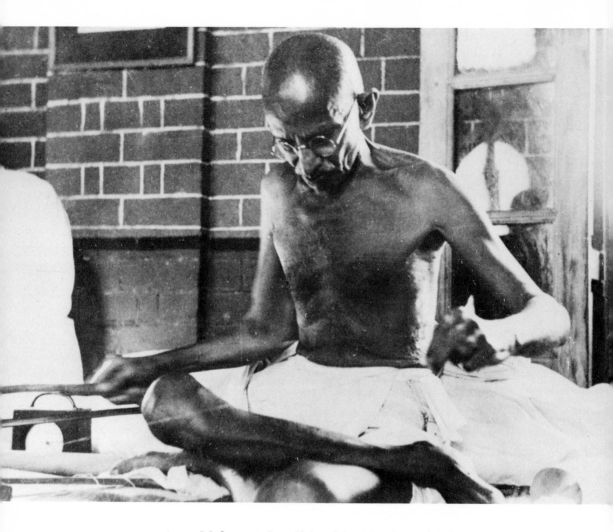

Mahatma Gandhi at his spinning wheel.
He popularized hand spinning on the theory
that it promoted self-sufficiency and
enabled one to identify with the poor.

Gandhi was not, however, successful in his fight to abolish Untouchability. He forced India's leaders to include the ban in the constitution—but one has only to visit India today to see that the bulk of the Hindus still consider these people less than human.

The caste system has been a part of the Hindu religion at least as far back as 1500 B.C. It is obviously so much a part of Hinduism that even a revered leader like Gandhi couldn't stamp it out.

SACRED SCRIPTURES
OF HINDUISM

The *Rig-Veda* is the oldest of the Hindu sacred writings. Some authorities think it originated as early as 3000 B.C. as oral chants of Aryan priests. It was first put into writing about 1000 B.C. It is believed to be the oldest religious book still used by a living religion.

The Vedas, which were brought to India in 1500 B.C. by the invading Aryans, are hymns to the Aryan gods. The Vedas also contain instructions for making sacrifices to these same gods—a ritual that is no longer used.

Indra, god of storm and war, was the chief Aryan god. Some of the hymns tell of his leadership in a mighty struggle between good and evil. Some Hindus today think this is a mixture of fact and myth. Indra, they say, was probably a real person and the leader of the Aryas that swept into India. The fighting may be a mystical account of the war between the invaders and the people of Mohenjo-Daro.

The Vedas are written in the ancient Sanskrit language. While few Hindus can read Sanskrit today, they learn to recite some verses during the *Brahma-yajna,* an act of worship carried on in the home.

THE BRAHMANAS

The Brahmanas are sacred prose writings that date back to about 600 B.C. They do not affect the average Hindu directly and are not read by the common people. The *Brahmanas* are instruction books for Brahmin priests.

They were written to help increase the importance of Brahmin priests in early Hindu society. Originally priests were not the highest caste in India. Their rise to this position came through the influence of the *Brahmanas* between 800 B.C. and 500 B.C. It was during this time that Indra lost his place as chief of the gods. He was replaced by the present trinity, Brahma, Vishnu and Siva.

THE UPANISHADS

The Aryans found an easier life in India. This gave them time for thought and study. They began asking questions about themselves, nature, the gods, and creation itself. They no longer believed in a wind god just because the wind blew. They now wanted explanations that gave logical answers to complex questions. This questioning of old beliefs grew into modern Hinduism.

These questions brought new ideas that were written into the *Upanishads,* compiled between 600 B.C. and 300 B.C. These writings give an explanation of the gods, and mankind, and present a plan of religious ideals that can provide a way to individual salvation. The *Upanishads* explain the Wheel of Life and the ways one may overcome karma to return to the Supreme Spirit from which the soul comes.

The *Upanishads* establish Brahman as the Supreme Spirit. Some sects claim Brahman is the only reality. All else is *maya* (illusion). Brahma, Vishnu and Siva, rebirth, dharma, karma, caste, and the other aspects of Hinduism all come from the authority of the *Upanishads*.

THE HINDU "NOAH"

These sacred writings are supported by the *Laws of Manu*. These were first put into a code about 250 B.C. and are rules for daily Hindu life. Manu, who made these laws, was the first man after the world was reborn. (According to Hinduism, the world is destroyed every 4,000,000,000 years. It is then reborn for another 4,000,000,000 years.)

Near the close of the previous world-life, Manu befriended a fish. This fish was actually an avatar of Brahma and warned Manu that a flood would destroy the world. Manu built a boat and took seven priests onto it with him.

The deluge came as Brahma predicted and the world was covered by water. Manu sailed for years, pulled along by fish. Finally the waters receded, and the boat was grounded on a mountain top. Manu went down to a plain after the water dried up. Here he began the work of restarting life for another 4,000,000,000 years.

He wrote the *Laws of Manu* to guide his people. His laws deal with old customs, government, rites to ask forgiveness, and general advice to mankind. Here is an example:

Strive to complete the task thou hast begun;
Wearied, renew thy efforts once again;
Again fatigued, once more the work begin;
So shalt thou earn success and fortune win.

In other words, if at first you don't succeed, try again.

THE RAMAYANA

The *Ramayana* is an epic poem. It tells the story of Prince Rama, who is really the seventh avatar of Vishnu.

Court jealousy drives Rama from his father's palace. His faithful wife Sita follows Rama into exile but is kidnapped by evil Ravana, the demon king of Sri Lanka (formerly Ceylon). Rama goes to rescue her, aided by the monkey king Hanuman. There is a great battle between good and evil. Rama defeats his enemy, rescues Sita, and becomes king upon the death of his father. After death, he reverts to his god-self Vishnu, and returns to his heaven.

On the surface the *Ramayana* is an exciting adventure story. What lifts it above the level of just a story is that it mirrors Hindu ideals. Rama is the perfect Hindu. Sita is the perfect Hindu wife. Devotion to duty, devotion to caste, and reverence for religious laws are all woven into the story. Some Hindus say that the story of Rama and Sita touches the heart more than any other story ever written.

THE MAHABHARATA

The *Mahabharata* is the second great Hindu epic, written sometime between 500 B.C. and 100 B.C. It is 220,000 lines along—the longest epic poem ever written.

It has been called a "sacred history," and is an encyclopedia in story form. It includes traditions, legends, history, ethics and philosophy. All this is told against a framework of wars that illustrate the struggle between good and evil.

THE BHAGAVAD-GITA

Bhagavad-Gita means "the Heavenly Song," and is a part of the *Mahabharata.* Today, however, it is often published as a separate book.

The *Bhagavad-Gita* teaches love of Krishna, the eighth and most beloved avatar of Vishnu. Krishna has sometimes been compared to Jesus Christ. Krishna certainly shared Christ's great love for humanity. And both were born on earth to bring comfort, deep wisdom, and divine love to mankind.

The *Gita,* as it is often called, is written in story form. It begins on the eve of a great battle between two armies. Krishna has refused to fight in the war. He agrees, however, to drive the chariot for Arjuna, one of the warrior heroes.

Arjuna begins to have doubts about fighting. Krishna talks to him of love of humanity, love of god, duty, caste, and reincarnation. In his discussion, he brings hope back to the despairing heart of Arjuna—and in doing so, he gives similar hope to all who read the *Bhagavad-Gita.*

A 17th century illustration of the epic poem Ramayana. *In this scene, Rama and his army are investigating a fortress.*

Mahatma Gandhi once told what the *Bhagavad-Gita* meant to him. In doing so, he summed up the feeling of the Hindu people toward this beautiful book. Gandhi said that when he was faced with heavy disappointments and there seemed no ray of hope anywhere, "I turn to the *Bhagavad-Gita* . . . and I immediately begin to smile in the midst of overwhelming sorrow. My life has been full of external tragedies. If they have not left any visible and indelible effect upon me, I owe it to the teachings of the *Bhagavad-Gita.*"

Over the years, many western writers and philosophers became familiar with the *Bhagavad-Gita.* The famous American essayist Ralph Waldo Emerson was fond of reading it, as was Henry David Thoreau. In *Walden,* Thoreau said, "In the morning I bathe my intellect in the stupendous philosophy of the *Bagavat Geeta* . . . in comparison with which our modern world and its literature seems puny and trivial."

Even without its spiritual qualities, the *Bhagavad-Gita* would still be read because of its beauty of language. However, the *Gita* is loved by so many people because it gives them hope. It was written at a time when Hinduism taught that each person was a slave to karma, and must work out his or her own sal-

Krishna, an avatar of Vishnu, is probably the most popular of Vishnu's many forms. This bronze statue of Krishna dancing was made sometime between the 12th and 14th centuries.

vation alone. With the *Bhagavad-Gita,* however, Krishna came and offered his help. A person struggling to overcome karma was no longer alone. He or she had someone filled with love who genuinely wanted to help people.

This is made clear in an important part of the Heavenly Song when Krishna says, "Even those who are of low and unpretending birth may find the path to higher happiness, if they depend on me. . . . Then be not sorrowful; from all thy sins I will deliver thee. Think thou on me."

Gandhi used this portion of the *Gita* in his arguments to accept the Untouchables as full members of the Indian society.

THE PURANAS
AND MYTHS

A Hindu is free to worship any one or all of the different gods. However, since many of these are avatars of either Vishnu or Siva, most Hindus are worshipping either Siva or Vishnu in one form or another.

This is true even when the personal god chosen is a goddess. Dr. Monier-Williams explains this: "The principle Hindu gods are supposed to possess a double nature—one quiet, the other active. The active, called his *Sakti,* is personified as his wife, or as the female half of his essence. These wives of the gods can take different forms. Siva's wife, for example, is *Jagan-matri,* Mother of the Universe, in one form. In another she is Kali, the Goddess of Destruction. She is also known as Parvati, Durga, and Uma in other aspects."

The gods are equal, but at one time their followers were jealous, each wanting his or her god to be the greater. This rivalry led to the writing of the *Puranas,* in about A.D. 500.

(31)

82-58

Those who follow Vishnu are Vaishnavites. The followers of Siva are called Shaivas. They do not come from any particular part of the country or any particular level of society. The only difference between the two groups is their choice of the god they follow.

THE GREATER GOD

There are eighteen *Puranas,* with six devoted to each of the gods, Brahma, Vishnu and Siva. They cover many points, but their main purpose is to prove the superiority of one god over another. One way this is done is shown in a story from the Vishnu *Sattvika Purana.*

Some wise men in ancient times argued over which god was the greater. They took the question to Bhrigu, one of the ten sages. Bhrigu did not know the answer, but agreed to test the gods to find out.

He went first to Brahma. Bhrigu purposely did not pay respect to the god. Brahma's wrath was terrible to behold.

Next, Bhrigu went to Siva. Again he failed to give the god his rightful respect. Siva was so angry that he would have killed the sage if Siva's wife had not begged for Bhrigu's life.

Finally Bhrigu went to Vishnu. He found the god asleep with his head in the lap of Lakshmi, his wife. Bhrigu kicked Vishnu to awaken the god. Instead of being angry, Vishnu begged the sage's pardon for putting him to the trouble of having to kick his god awake. He then gently massaged Bhrigu's foot, which was bruised from kicking Vishnu.

The sage then reported back to the wise men that Vishnu

was the greatest of the gods. "He overpowers by the greatest of all weapons," he said. "This is gentleness and generosity."

A DARKER SIDE OF HINDUISM

Much of Hinduism involves the all-embracing love of Vishnu, but there is a darker side. This is one form of Siva worship. One person may withdraw to live a hermit's life of devout meditation. Others may torture their flesh or hold their limbs in a certain position until they grow in that manner. Some may even lie on beds of nails.

These people, called ascetics, claim their actions teach people about the power obtained by suppressing the desires of the body. This, they believe, leads to the highest spiritual knowledge.

Another form of Shaivism is the worship of Durga, an avatar of Siva's wife. Durga is the Goddess of Terror, and has been described as a terrible person who delights in blood. Yet, in times of great distress, when humanity was threatened by monsters, Durga came to earth to fight for mankind.

In still another form, Siva's wife is worshipped as Kali, the most terrible form of all. In ancient times she demanded human sacrifices. Today, those who worship her satisfy her hunger for blood by sacrificing small animals.

TEMPLE WORSHIP OF SIVA

In contrast to the darker side of Siva, the worship of the god in his own temple is quiet, pure and austere. No food offerings are brought to him as they are for Vishnu. The stone images of the god are reverently washed with water from a sacred river. Then flowers are presented.

WORSHIP IN VISHNU'S TEMPLES

Daily worship in Vishnu's temples is much different from that of Siva. The worship is often directed to Vishnu's avatars, Krishna and Rama. Priests wash the images of the gods each day. Incense and candles are burned before them. Food offerings are placed in front of the images, but the gods take only the spirit of the food. The food can then be eaten by the worshippers as a blessing with healing powers. Flowers, and sometimes gifts, are often brought as well.

REFORMERS

All religions have their protestants—those who protest about some part of the religion's doctrine. This often leads to new sects and even new religions.

HINDUISM AND BUDDHISM

The most famous Hindu protestant was Prince Siddartha Gautama, who became The Buddha. Siddartha lived from 563 B.C. to 483 B.C. He became dissatisfied with life in the royal palace, and gave it up to become a wandering beggar, following the Hindu ascetic life for six years. He failed to find the salvation he sought, and gradually formed his own ideas. These developed into Buddhism, now one of the world's great religions with about 250 million followers.

The Buddha agreed with Hinduism—that the world is a place of misery. He accepted karma, rebirth, and moksha (release from the Wheel of Life), but he rejected all gods. Instead of the soul returning to Brahma, the Buddha said it went to *nirvana,* a place of eternal bliss within the spirit of the universe. He also rejected the caste system. All people were equal in his sight.

Although one of the world's great religions, Buddhism has almost disappeared from the land of its birth. The original Buddhism was strict, austere, and required a follower to live a monastic life. The rise of the Siva cults promised an easier way to salvation than either the old Hinduism or the original Buddhism. This drew followers away from Buddhism.

THE JAIN REFORM

Mahavira was another who used Hinduism as a base for a new religion. Mahavira, born in 599 B.C., was a member of the warrior class. His caste was envious of the Brahmins who were named the first class in the Vedas. Mahavira denied the Vedas. His ideas eventually developed into Jainism.

The Jains believe the soul is imprisoned in the body. This creates karma, which causes rebirths until the soul can free itself from worldly sins. Only Jain monks, who sacrifice worldly possessions and ways, can hope for salvation. Not everyone can do this, due to family duties. So many Jains lead a normal life. They gain some merit to help their next rebirth by feeding and aiding the monks.

Jainism does not have a large following in India today. But it is important because so many Jains are in control of industries and financial institutions.

SIKHISM

Sikhism grew from the ideas of Nanak, who was born in A.D. 1469. India was then under the conquering Moslem Moguls. Nanak was inspired by previous attempts to bring the Moslem and Hindu religions together.

At first, Nanak tried to do the same thing. He took the best parts of the two religions to make a new faith. This failed to attract worshippers. He then created Sikhism, by combining Hindu *bhakti*—loving devotion to a personal god—with Moslem Sufism, a mystic Islamic sect. Today, there are over one million followers of Sikhism.

SOME OTHER REFORMERS

There has been a steady parade of Hindu reformers. None altered the basic religion, but some made important changes.

One of these was Ram Mohan Roy, who died in 1833. Roy was a Brahmin whose faith was shaken when he saw his sister-in-law burned on her husband's funeral pyre. This ancient custom was called *suttee*. The British, then in control of India, had done nothing to stop it. Roy began a campaign against suttee and finally had it abolished.

BRAHMO SAMAJ

In 1826 Roy founded the *Brahmo-Samaj* (Society of God). In this worship, Roy added features he found in his studies of Islam and Christianity. Roy worked hard for social reform. For instance, up to this time women were the subjects of their husbands. The ideal Hindu woman lived only for the welfare of her husband and her family. While a few sometimes became wandering monks, a woman normally gained the merit needed for her karma through religious devotion and by being a devout Hindu wife and mother. Roy worked hard to raise the social status of women, abolish childhood marriages, and to change the caste system.

RAMAKRISHNA

Gadadhar Chattopadhyaya was a priest of Kali, an avatar of Siva. He broke away from Shaivism to form his own sect. His followers came to call him Ramakrishna, combining the names of Rama and Krishna, the two most beloved avatars of Vishnu.

Ramakrishna studied both Islam and Christianity. He had visions in which he saw Christ, Krishna and Mohammed. These visions convinced him that all religions are true. He explained this by saying that fish will taste differently if cooked in different ways. He meant that if different religions are stripped of their rituals and practices, they are basically the same.

HINDU CULTURE
AND CUSTOMS

India is a beautiful country steeped in history, tradition, and art. Today it is also overcrowded, poor, and constantly swept by devastating epidemics, floods, and violent storms. For the 85 percent of the Indian population that follows Hinduism, religion is what makes life endurable. Hinduism teaches them that their plight in life has been caused by their actions in the life they lived before. But, regardless of the misery one may find in this life, Hinduism provides hope that the next life will be better.

Hinduism is taught from the cradle and is engrained in its followers. In addition, Hindu customs and culture are deeply rooted in the religion. Indian literature and art through the ages have drawn their greatest inspiration from Hinduism. It also affects the country's festivals and inspires the pilgrimages that Hindus love to make. In effect, Hinduism provides each person a roadmap to follow through one's entire life.

THE STAGES OF HINDU LIFE

Regardless of the sect one follows, the ideal Hindu's existence follows the "Four Stages of Life." These stages were first set forth in Vedic times, but did not become part of Hindu culture until A.D. 100. They were to apply only to men, for a woman's place was still considered to be bound up in her home.

THE FIRST STAGE

The first stage of Hindu life is that of a student. This stage generally lasts through youth. The child or young man is supposed to study and undergo twelve religious rites. Today, however, some of the twelve are skipped.

The most important of these rites—for the first three castes —is initiation into the ranks of the "twice born." This sacred ceremony, called *Upanayana,* signifies that a Hindu boy is now ready to take up his serious religious duties. It can be compared in principle to the Judaic Bar Mitzvah. A Brahmin child takes the rites when he is eight years old. A Kshatriya (warrior caste) boy is twice-born at eleven. The Vaisya (merchant caste) boy is initiated when he is twelve. Children of the working class cannot be twice-born and do not observe this rite.

Today there are religious schools, which the young men at-

Women climb the steps to worship at a Hindu temple in New Delhi, India's capital city.

tend. In older times boys went to live with their *gurus* (religious teachers) who became second fathers to them. Those who could not afford to live away from home were taught by wandering monks who went from house to house.

Stage one ends with the young man's marriage.

THE SECOND STAGE

A Hindu man is expected to marry and raise a family. During this second stage of life, he continues his religious devotions—but his primary responsibility is to provide for his family. This includes seeing that his sons are given religious training in the first stage of their lives.

Until recently the Hindu wife was uneducated, except in household and family duties. She did have considerable influence in the home and was often the driving force behind the family's religious activity. The position of Hindu women is improving, but very slowly.

THE THIRD STAGE

When a Hindu grows old and has sons to carry on his business, he has fulfilled his family duties. He may then leave home alone, or in a group, to devote himself to religious practices and experiences. This is called *vanaprasthya*.

In this stage he is preparing himself for death. Some sects permit a man to take his wife with him on these pilgrimages. Very occasionally, a woman may undertake these pilgrimages alone.

Some sects do not demand that a man leave home in this stage. However, he must withdraw from all family duties in order to devote himself entirely to religious devotions. At this time his oldest son takes over responsibility for the family.

THE FINAL STAGE

Having prepared himself for death in the third stage, the old man must renounce all worldly possessions in the final state. He keeps only a bowl for the food he begs, a pot for his drinking water, and a loin cloth to wear. He withdraws from society to live as a hermit until he dies.

Only the most religious follow through all four stages. Most are content with only the first two. Some may go into the third stage, but very few today take up the hermit life of the fourth stage.

LOVE OF ANIMALS

Hindus have a great love for animals. This is partly due to their belief in reincarnation. An animal may once have been an unknown man, a woman, or even a relative in a past life.

A number of animals have become minor Hindu gods because of some service to Brahma, Vishnu or Siva. One of the best loved of these is Hanuman, the monkey king, who aided Rama in the *Ramayana*. Another animal god is Ganesha, "the elephant-headed," who is the lord of wisdom. Garuda—half-man, half-bird—is the flying mount that Vishnu rides. Jambavan, king of the bears, also fought for Rama.

Horses were never worshipped, although the greatest sacrifice a king could offer in Vedic days was that of a horse. A horse with proper markings was turned loose to wander where it wished for an entire year. Soldiers followed to protect it, but could not interfere with its freedom of movement. At the end of the year the horse was returned and sacrificed.

WORSHIP OF THE COW

Hindus believe the cow is the most sacred animal. Therefore, the killing of a cow is one of the gravest religious crimes. It is not, however, a civil crime—although Hindus have been pressing for such a law.

Cows are permitted to roam freely through city streets. On several occasions angry mobs have attacked foreign drivers who have accidentally killed a sacred cow.

Cow worship began in Vedic times. The cow was a very valuable animal to nomadic herdsmen. It provided milk, and its butter was made into *ghee*—an oil still used widely in India. In addition, it was the mother of the oxen that pulled carts and worked fields.

A street scene in Calcutta, the most densely populated city of India. Cows are sacred animals to Hindus, and can often be seen roaming freely in the streets.

WORSHIP IN THE HOME

While Hindus sometimes worship in temples, most of their worship is done at home before shrines to the god or gods of the family's choice.

The family worship includes the five *Maha-yajnas* or great acts of worship. These are:

1. Recitation of a passage from a Veda. This fulfills the requirement of reverence for the Vedas and is called *Brahma-yajna* —worship of Brahman.
2. Worship of departed ancestors by putting out offerings of water, and by performing funeral rites.
3. Worship of the gods with morning or evening offerings or sacrifices. This is called *Deva-yajna*—god worship.
4. Worship of all things—*Bhuta-yajna*—which is done by scattering rice grains or a similar food outside the door. This is an offering to small animals, birds and insects. It is accompanied by a prayer, part of which goes: "May the ants, worms, insects, and whoever are hungry, receive this food offered by me."
5. Worship of people—*Manushya-yajna*—is satisfied by hospitality to one's guests.

The devout Hindu has three *Sandhyas* (private religious services) that take place at sunrise, midday, and sunset.

FESTIVALS

Hindus love to get together at festivals. One of the most famous is Holi. According to legend, this festival was set aside by Brahma for the lower classes and it is still their most popular

The Hindu festival of Kumbha Mela
takes place once every twelve years.
At the festival in 1974,
four million Indians came to bathe
in the holy waters of the Ganges River.

holiday. It comes according to the lunar calendar in either February or March.

Local customs vary, but the festival is often loud and unrestrained. There is dancing in the streets, where people dress in many-hued clothes and throw dyed water on each other. Tricks are played, and ceremonial fires are lighted to popular gods.

JAGANNATH

Another famous festival is that of Jagannath, held at a temple in Puri, east India. Jagannath is believed to be an avatar of Vishnu. His name is the source of the English word "juggernaut," meaning something that forces blind devotion of great sacrifice.

A statue of Jagannath is pulled through the streets in a gigantic cart by hundreds of worshippers. In times past, worshippers were sometimes so overcome by the sight of the god that they threw themselves under the giant wheels of his cart. They believed this sacrifice destroyed their sins. This is now forbidden by law.

PILGRIMAGES

There is no lack of places to worship anywhere in India. However, Hindus love pilgrimages. They believe that it shows great respect to travel a great distance to worship a god.

There is even one festival that is built around travel. Four sacred places are visited during one tour. All the sites are situated on rivers. The faithful bathe in the streams, dip seeds in the water to ensure a good crop, and pray for strong sons.

Bathing ghats *on the banks of the Ganges in the holy city of Banaras. These platforms enable people to wash away their sins in the sacred waters of the river.*

There is much merrymaking at this festival, which takes place every three years.

BANARAS

The sacred city of Banaras, on the Ganges River between Delhi and Calcutta, is popular among pilgrims. It has been renamed Varanasi, but is also still known by its old name.

Banaras (or Varanasi), in its different way, is to Hindus what Jerusalem is to Jews and Christians—and what Mecca is to Moslems.

A 36-mile (58-km) road circles the most sacred parts of the city. Walking this road (a symbol of the Wheel of Life) brings great merit to the pilgrim. Some sects believe that if the dying are carried along this road all their sins will be forgiven.

Banaras has thousands of temples. A member of just about any sect can find a temple in which to worship alone, or with the aid of priests. There are also guides to direct the faithful through the sacred parts of the city.

The most important part of the pilgrimage is to bathe in the waters of the Ganges River. The river banks are jammed with temples with stone steps leading to the water. Ceremonial bathing, which followers believe will wash sins away, is held in the early morning.

Banaras is especially sacred to followers of Siva, since it is said that this god once worked miracles here.

HINDUISM TODAY

Hinduism continues to grow due mainly to the constant increase in the Indian population. The high birth rate adds 13 million people a year to an already crowded country.

The majority of Hindus live in India, which is 85 percent Hindu. There has not been a large foreign conversion to this religion. The 1977 estimate places about 75,000 Hindu followers in North America—of which many are immigrants from India. South America has 533,000; Europe 350,000; Africa 490,500; and Oceania (islands of the Pacific) 640,000. Asia has over 500 million. Most Western foreigners who convert to Eastern religions seem to prefer Buddhism.

Hinduism, because of its strong belief in karma and dharma, has been slow to meet world demands for social changes. The changes that have occurred came only after the strongest pressures.

Women's rights have improved slowly. In 1955–56, for the first time civil law changes permitted women to obtain divorces, to inherit property, and to enjoy more social justice. Caste discrimination was abolished in the constitution of 1947, but still occurs today. It is too deeply embedded in Hinduism to be easily uprooted.

THE OLDEST RELIGION

All religions trace their origins to the beginning of time. Historically, many authorities believe Hinduism to be the world's oldest religion. In fact, Hinduism is a foreign word. Hindus call it *Santana Dharma,* the Eternal Religion. It began in pre-Vedic days long before the Aryans left their ancestral home to spread over Asia and Europe. The Vedas are the oldest sacred texts of any religion.

Hinduism's long life is due to its flexibility. It has so many sects that any person can find a place in it somewhere. If people believe in the Triad (Brahma, Vishnu, and Siva), caste, karma, dharma, the Vedas, and reincarnation, they are Hindus, regardless of how much their sect may vary from another.

HINDUISM'S FUTURE

Hindus have always shown remarkable devotion to their religion. Not even the Christians under the Roman emperors suffered more than the Hindus under some of their Mogul conquerors. The Moguls ruled India from 1519 until the British conquest in the eighteenth century.

India was granted independence from Great Britain in 1947. At that time the Moslem minority in India feared being governed by the Hindus. This resulted in the present division of the country into India, and the Moslem nation of Pakistan. Pakistan later divided again, with eastern Pakistan becoming Bangladesh.

Hinduism continues to grow, and its hold upon the people is as strong as ever. It can be expected to become more conscious of social needs and changes in time. This, however, will undoubtedly come slowly, because history shows that changes have never been rapid in India.

IMPORTANT DATES IN THE HISTORY OF HINDUISM

2300 B.C.   Golden age of Mohenjo-Daro.

1500 B.C.   Aryans invade India and destroy Mohenjo-Daro.

1000 B.C.   *Rig-Veda,* oldest of Hindu sacred writings, set down from older oral accounts.

600 B.C.   Brahmanas written (instruction manuals for priests).

600 B.C.   Earliest date given for Laws of Manu. Some authorities put the writing of the laws as much as 300 years later.

528 B.C.   Buddha preaches his first sermon, beginning Buddhism, the most important of the religions that formed from Hinduism.

500 B.C.   One date given for the earliest form of the *Mahabharata* and the *Ramayana,* Hindu poetic epics.

A.D. 1023   Mahmud raids India, destroying Hindu temples.

A.D. 1519   Babur, a Moslem conqueror, establishes Mogul rule in India, leading to great oppression of the Hindus.

A.D. 1557   British begin conquest of India.

A.D. 1947   British rule ends in India. New Indian constitution outlaws "Untouchability." Pakistan formed because Moslems refused to live under a Hindu government.

A.D. 1950   New laws ease some Hindu restrictions on women's rights.

Note: All B.C. dates are controversial and not accepted by all scholars.

GLOSSARY

Aryan   The Indo-European language spoken by a prehistoric people who called themselves Aryas. This language is the root of most European languages.

Atman   The Hindu term for soul.

Avatar   The reincarnation (rebirth) of a Hindu god in an earthly body. This rebirth is made for the love of humanity and to help mankind find the way to salvation.

Bhagavad-Gita   The name means "the Heavenly (or Celestial) Song," and is a summation of Hindu ideals and religion. The ideals are set forth in the words of Vishnu as comfort for a man who has doubts during a war between good and evil forces. The *Bhagavad-Gita* is considered to be one of the most beautiful religious books ever written.

Bhakti   Loving devotion to a personal god.

Brahma   One of the three chief gods of Hinduism, all of whom were created by Brahman, the supreme spirit of the universe. Brahman is known as the Creator of Life.

Brahman   The supreme spirit of the universe.

Dharma   Highest Hindu spiritual law.

Guru   A Hindu religious teacher. In times past, a Hindu boy went to live with his guru until he was old enough to marry.

Jainism   A religion based upon Hinduism, but which resembles Buddhism. Jainism teaches reverence for its wise men and respect for all living things. A Jain may not kill even an insect, for even it has life.

Karma   The effect of one's good and bad deeds in a lifetime. Karma is what causes the soul to be reborn on earth. A bad karma results in a bad future life, but a good karma means a better future life.

Lingam   Image of the god Siva in the form of the male sex organ.

Mahabharata   An epic Hindu poem, written around the literary frame of wars that personify the struggle between good and evil.

Moksha   Moksha is release from the cycle of rebirths. The soul achieving moksha does not have to be born again, but rejoins Brahman for eternal bliss and happiness.

Rama   The legendary hero of the epic, *The Ramayana*. Rama was an avatar (rebirth) of the god Vishnu. He is the Hindu ideal of a man.

Ramayana   The epic poem that tells the story of Rama, the ideal Hindu man. On the surface the *Ramayana* is an exciting adventure story of Rama's search for his wife who has been abducted by the demon king of Sri Lanka, but by describing Rama's life the epic presents Hindu ideals.

Rig-Veda   First and most important of the Vedas, the earliest Hindu sacred writings.

Saivism   Hindu sect devoted to worship of the god Siva.

Samsara   The Hindu Wheel of Life; continual rebirth after deaths.

Siva   One of the Hindu Triad of gods, with Brahma and Vishnu. He is called the Destroyer of Life. Siva is worshipped in different forms, including worship through his wives, Kali and Durga.

Upanishads   Early religious writings that defined the basic beliefs of Hinduism. The Upanishads define karma, reincarnation, dharma, caste, and the other basic beliefs that one must accept to be a Hindu.

Vishnu   One of the three major Hindu gods. Vishnu is called the Preserver of Life. His avatar Krishna, who appears in the *Bhagavad-Gita,* is the most beloved of all Hindu personal gods. Vishnu's outstanding characteristic is his love of humanity.

Vedas   The earliest of all Hindu sacred writings. The Vedas were originally chanted as hymns to the Aryan gods. A belief in the Vedas is one of the requirements for a person to be a Hindu.

Yoga   A Hindu religious belief that teaches how to obtain union with Brahman through meditation. Meditation is aided by certain body positions and recitation of the mystic word *Om.*

FOR FURTHER READING

Bothwell, Jean. *The First Book of India*. New York: Franklin Watts, Inc., 1971.

Chandavarkar, Sumana. *Children of India*. New York: Lothrop, Lee & Shepherd Co., 1971.

Fairservis, Walter, Jr. *India*. Cleveland: World Publishing Co., 1961.

Shetty, Sharat. *A Hindu Boyhood*. New York: M. Evans & Co., 1970.

Wolcott, Leonard and Carolyn. *Religions Around the World*. Nashville and New York: Abingdon Press, 1967.

INDEX